TREASURES FROM
SUTTON HOO

Gareth Williams

THE BRITISH MUSEUM PRESS

© 2011 The Trustees of the British Museum

Gareth Williams has asserted the right to be identified as
the author of this work

First published in 2011 by The British Museum Press
A division of The British Museum Company Ltd
The British Museum
Great Russell Street, London WC1B 3DG

britishmuseum.org/publishing

Reprinted 2014, 2015, 2019, 2021

A catalogue record for this book is available from the British Library

ISBN: 978-0-7141-2825-2

Designed by Zoë Mellors
Maps by David Hoxley
Printed in the UK by Kingsbury Press

The majority of the objects illustrated in this book are from the collection
of the British Museum. Their museum registration numbers are listed on
page 48. Further information about the Museum and its collection can be
found at www.britishmuseum.org.

CONTENTS

INTRODUCTION

In May 1939 the archaeologist Basil Brown discovered an Anglo-Saxon ship burial at Sutton Hoo, near Woodbridge in Suffolk. The wonderful objects buried in the ship were still there waiting to be found. Seventy years later, despite all the discoveries made since, the Sutton Hoo ship burial remains one of the most important finds in British archaeology, and one of the greatest treasures in the British Museum.

The importance of the find comes partly from the striking appearance of the objects. The iconic helmet in particular provides the one identifiable 'face' of the Anglo-Saxons. More than any other object, it has come to symbolize the period which many people refer to unjustly as the 'Dark Ages', between the end of Roman Britain shortly after AD 400 and the writing of the first history of England in AD 732.

After decades of study and thousands of words in print, there are still many things we do not know for certain about the burial. The blank stare of the helmet prompts the biggest unanswered question: who was buried in the ship at Sutton Hoo, and what was the significance of the beautiful objects with which he was buried?

Opposite: Iron helmet from the Sutton Hoo ship burial. H. 31.8 cm (max)

DISCOVERY AND EXCAVATION

In 1938 a Suffolk landowner, Mrs Edith Pretty, invited a local archaeologist, Basil Brown, to investigate what lay beneath a group of obviously man-made mounds on her estate at Sutton Hoo. On excavating three of the mounds, Brown found that they had been disturbed and, although they still contained recognizable Anglo-Saxon objects, only fragments of grave-goods survived. The two smaller mounds contained cremation burials, and only a few related objects.

The larger mound, Mound 2, proved more exciting. Although the acidic nature of the soil had destroyed much of the organic material in the grave, Brown recognized rusty ship rivets in the ground, and realized that he had discovered the robbed remains of an Anglo-Saxon ship burial. It contained fragments of a sword, a glass vessel, silver-gilt mounts from drinking horns and a silver

buckle, all of which showed that it had once been a very wealthy burial. Better still was yet to come.

The following summer, Brown returned at the invitation of Mrs Pretty to excavate the largest mound, Mound 1. This also showed signs of disturbance, and broken pottery in a pit indicated that robbers had dug into the top of the mound in the sixteenth or early

Above: Burial mounds at Mrs Pretty's Sutton Hoo estate.

seventeenth century. Fortunately, it turned out that they had missed their prize.

Brown had again discovered ship rivets. By leaving these in place and carefully excavating down to them, he was able to uncover the full shape of the ship. This was shown both by the rivets and by the impression of the ship in the sand, although the wood itself had long rotted away. Altogether, the ship was around twenty-seven metres long and four and a half metres wide. Unlike Mound 2, Mound 1 contained an undisturbed burial chamber within the ship.

While Brown was uncovering the ship, Charles Phillips, an archaeologist from Cambridge University, visited the site. Like Brown, Phillips recognized that a hugely important discovery had been made and drew it to the attention of the authorities. The Office of Works, at that time the government department responsible for archaeology, took charge of the excavation, which was to be overseen by Phillips, although Brown remained as his assistant. Phillips assembled a team of skilled archaeologists to excavate the burial chamber, while a team from the Science Museum recorded the ship.

In the second half of July 1939 the burial chamber was excavated, revealing first fragments of iron and wood, then silver dishes, gold buckles and ornaments (some decorated with garnets and glass), weapons and armour, a purse of gold coins, a cauldron, drinking vessels and traces of textiles.

An inquest was held on 14 August to establish whether the find was Treasure Trove, in which case it would be the property of the Crown. Under the law of the time, only goods buried with the intention of later recovery constituted Treasure Trove. As a grave, the Sutton Hoo burial did not fit this description, and the finds were declared to be the property of Mrs Pretty. However, she

Above: Portrait of Mrs Edith Pretty.

Opposite: Archaeologists unearth the shoulder-clasps, as Mrs Pretty looks on.

quickly gave them to the nation, in one of the most generous single donations ever made to a museum.

With the Second World War looming, the finds spent the next few years hidden in the London Underground, together with other objects from the British Museum's collection. The burial itself was covered with bracken, but not refilled. During the war, many of the detailed records of the ship were destroyed, although very clear photographs survived.

Above: One of the shoulder-clasps in the soil.

Opposite: The impression of the ship is revealed.

The delay caused by the war meant that Mrs Pretty, who died in 1942, never knew exactly what she had found. Research began after the war under the direction of a young British Museum curator, Rupert Bruce-Mitford, who led a project that culminated in a massive three-volume account of the burial published between 1975 and 1983. This included a partial re-excavation of the site, which revealed human occupation at Sutton Hoo since prehistoric times.

An even more ambitious research project was directed by Professor Martin Carver of York University between 1983 and 1993. This included a survey of the wider landscape around Sutton Hoo, as well as reinvestigation of the mounds already uncovered, and the excavation of several more, showing that the cemetery was in use between the late sixth and late seventh centuries. Carver's excavations also showed that the site had then been used for executions until the eleventh century: two groups of execution burials were discovered, with some of the bodies preserved as ghostly outlines in the sand.

Opposite: Reinvestigation of the site in the 1980s, directed by Professor Martin Carver.

Below: A 'sand body' found at the site.

13

CHAPTER 2

THE KINGDOM OF THE EAST ANGLES

The Anglo-Saxons were not a single people, but a loose grouping

of tribes and peoples who came from what is today southern

Scandinavia, northern Germany and the Netherlands.

Although we call them Anglo-Saxons for convenience, the term was first used at the end of the ninth century AD, shortly before England became a single kingdom for the first time. Their move to England took place gradually over a long period, and probably began in the fourth century AD.

At that time, Germanic warriors provided one of the main sources of soldiers for the Roman army, but they were also one of the main threats to the Roman Empire. A network of coastal forts in eastern England was known as the 'Saxon Shore', and Saxons at different times were probably both garrisons and potential invaders. As the Roman Empire collapsed in the fifth century, the first Anglo-Saxon settlers in England were probably mercenary

Left: Kingdoms in England
in the seventh century.

Key dates

c. 410	Conventional date for the end of Roman Britain.
c. 450	Britons unsuccessfully request Roman help against Anglo-Saxon invaders.
c. 450–550	Settlement of much of southern and eastern England by Angles and Saxons.
By 571	Wuffa, ancestor of the 'Wuffing' dynasty, is king of the East Angles.
c. 578	Tytila becomes king of the East Angles.
597	Arrival of St Augustine in Kent.
c. 599	Rædwald becomes king of the East Angles.
604	Bishop Mellitus converts King Sæberht of the East Saxons.
c. 600–610	Eadwine of Deira forced into exile by Æthelfrith of Bernicia.
c. 617	Rædwald defeats and kills Æthelfrith of Bernicia at the River Idle, but his own son Rægenhere is killed at the same battle. Rædwald is established firmly as over-king south of the Humber. Eadwine becomes king of Deira and Bernicia.
c. 624	Death of Rædwald. His son Eorpwald becomes king of the East Angles. Eadwine becomes the dominant Anglo-Saxon king, and is converted to Christianity.
627	Eorpwald killed by Ricberht.
633	Eadwine killed by Cadwallon of Gwynedd and Penda of Mercia.
c. 629–c. 634	Sigeberht, brother of Eorpwald, is king of the East Angles before retiring to a monastery.
c. 634	Ecgric, kinsman of Sigeberht, becomes king of the East Angles.
c. 636	Both Sigeberht and Ecgric are killed in battle against Penda of Mercia. Anna, nephew of Rædwald, becomes king of the East Angles.
654	Anna killed in battle.

troops in the pay of local rulers, trying to maintain an element of Roman authority.

Over the course of the fifth and sixth centuries, increasing numbers of people came to England from the Anglo-Saxon homelands. Graves show that this turned into a large-scale migration, with not only warriors but whole families arriving. The native British population (who spoke an early form of Welsh) were conquered by the Anglo-Saxon invaders. By the end of the seventh century these peoples had taken control of most of England, with the British maintaining control only in the north-west and south-west of the country, and in Wales.

Below: The Wilton Cross, found in Norfolk. Anglo-Saxon, AD 675–700. Gold and garnet pendant, set with an early Byzantine coin. H. 4.7 cm

Some Romano-British kingdoms survived long enough for their identities to be taken over by the new Anglo-Saxon rulers. These included Bernicia in the north-east, Deira (modern North and East Yorkshire), Lindsey (Lincolnshire) and Kent. Others took their names from small groups known as *sæte*. Their legacy survives today in names such as Somerset and Dorset. Other early kingdoms took their names from the two main peoples, the Angles and the Saxons.

Among the largest and most powerful of these was the kingdom of the East Angles, preserved today in the name East Anglia; the modern county names of Norfolk and Suffolk retain an earlier division of 'North Folk' and 'South Folk'. Early settlements developed in pockets in coastal areas and along the main river valleys. This meant that within the kingdom of the East Angles there were separate concentrations in East Norfolk, West

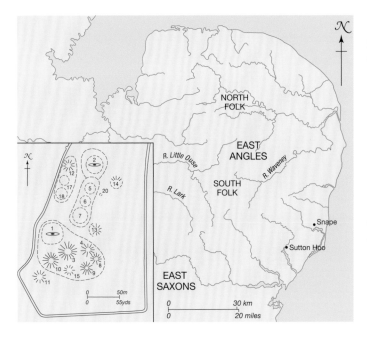

Left: Map of early Anglo-Saxon
East Anglia (inset: the numbered
burial mounds at the Sutton Hoo
cemetery).

Below: Silver penny of Aethelberht
with wolf and twins on the reverse.
Minted in East Anglia, c. AD 794.
Diam. 1.8 cm

Suffolk (along the Ouse and the Lark) and East Suffolk, around Ipswich and Woodbridge. To the south, the East Saxons (Essex) formed a separate kingdom from the Stour along the Thames estuary.

The location of Sutton Hoo on the river Deben suggests that the cemetery was close to an early centre of power in East Suffolk. The cemetery appears to have begun in the late sixth century, and to have reached its peak in the early seventh century. This matches the period in which the kingdom of the East Angles emerges for the first time in historical sources, and the cemetery is usually interpreted as the royal burial ground of the early kings of the East Angles.

17

CHAPTER 3

THE SUTTON HOO
SHIP BURIAL

The ship burial found in Mound 1 stands out from the other burials at Sutton Hoo in terms of the scale and splendour of the grave-goods. This is partly a reflection of fashion. The cemetery was in use over several generations, and both at Sutton Hoo and elsewhere (see chapter 5) the taste for elaborate burials was at its height in the first half of the seventh century. This was also a period in which gold was readily available, and a high point in the production of beautiful metalwork.

There is also a question of chance. The burial in Mound 1 was undisturbed, whereas most of the others had been at least partially robbed. The Mound 2 ship burial may have been as well equipped as this one, but we will never know for sure. Even so, compared with burials elsewhere, the Sutton Hoo ship burial is particularly

Above: Europe in the seventh century.

rich. Together with items that have been interpreted as 'regalia' (symbols of royal status), its wealth points to it being the grave of a king.

There are two main interpretations of why the treasures were placed in the grave. Traditionally, grave-goods represented the items which a dead person would need to 'live' in comfort in the afterlife. More recently, archaeologists have suggested that

Above: Half-sized replica of the ship found in Mound 1 at sail.

the choice of grave-goods had more to do with symbolizing the social status and perhaps the personal characteristics of the deceased when he or she had still been alive. Both explanations could be true at the same time. Either way, it is important to remember that the dead did not bury themselves, and that the selection of what went with them was made by those who buried them.

The ship burial

The treasure was buried within a chamber around five and a half metres by four and a half metres, placed in the centre of a ship around twenty-seven metres long. The ship was clinker-built (with overlapping planks), a style common across northern Europe in this period. Many of the best examples come from Scandinavia, and there are examples of ship burials in Scandinavia from the same period as Sutton Hoo and through to the early tenth century. There are also smaller examples of later Viking boat-burials in Britain and Ireland.

This does not mean that Sutton Hoo was a Viking burial. Instead it is a reminder that the Anglo-Saxons had their origins in southern Scandinavia, and that they continued to have contacts there after they settled in England. This is also shown by some of the grave-goods. The great Anglo-Saxon poem *Beowulf*, which includes a ship-funeral and references to just the sort of high-status items that appear in the grave, is largely set in southern Sweden and Denmark.

The ship was designed for rowing, with twenty to forty oars in total. These are not preserved, and nor are the rowlocks that would have held them. The rowers would also have formed part

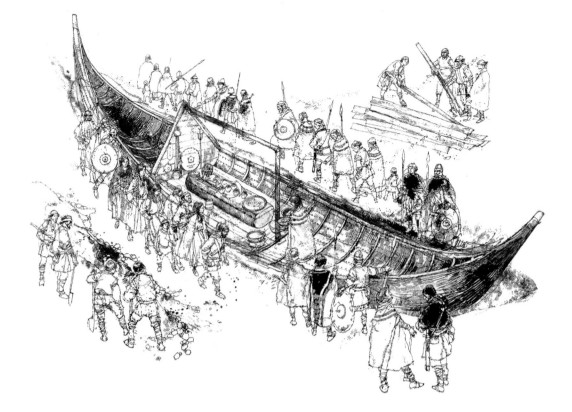

of their leader's war-band. No traces remain of fittings for a mast, but these would have been where the burial chamber was placed, and may have been either removed or obscured. Experiments with a half-sized replica of the ship show that it could have been sailed very effectively.

The burial chamber apparently had vertical walls at either end, with a sloping roof coming down to meet the sides of the ship. The position of individual items in the grave suggests that items were stacked against or hung from the end walls. In the centre, the body was placed in a wooden coffin, with further grave-goods inside, and more piled on the top. The various items reflect different aspects of the dead man's status.

Above: Artist's impression of the day of burial at Mound 1.

Above: Reconstruction of the shield from the Sutton Hoo ship burial, incorporating some original gold and garnet, copper-alloy and iron fittings. Diam. 91.4 cm

Far left: Iron sword with gold and cloisonné garnet fittings, from the Sutton Hoo ship burial. L. 31.8 cm

Left: Reconstruction of the pattern-welded sword blade.

The warrior-lord

Anglo-Saxon weapon burials are relatively common, but few contain more than two weapons, plus a simple shield. By contrast, the Sutton Hoo burial was very well equipped with both weapons and armour. Propped against the west wall of the burial chamber were five thrusting-spears, three throwing-spears, and a magnificent shield decorated with gold ornaments, some with additional garnets, together with gilt-bronze fittings to reinforce the rim of the shield. The elaborate decoration would never have stood up to use in battle, and it looks more like a symbol of warrior status than a functional protection.

Above: Reconstruction drawing of the sword-belt.

Below: Gold and garnet fittings from the scabbard and sword-belt from the Sutton Hoo ship burial. L. 7.3 cm (longest)

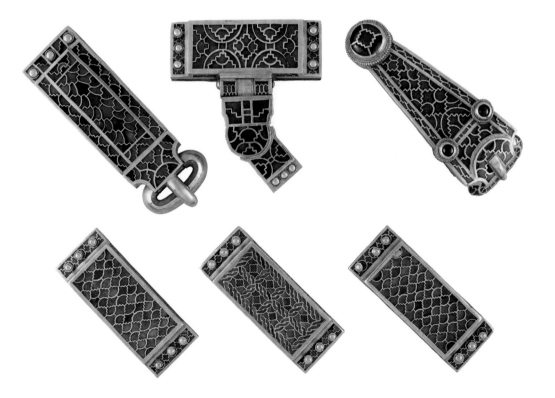

The warrior was probably buried in a coffin and the remaining war gear placed in and on top of it: a single spear, perhaps a favourite since it is separate from the others; a richly ornamented sword; a mail shirt; and the iconic Sutton Hoo helmet. The mail shirt is almost without parallel in an Anglo-Saxon context, made of alternate links of riveted and butted mail, only eight millimetres in diameter, providing strong yet flexible protection.

The sword was pattern-welded, meaning that the blade was fashioned from bundles of twisted rods hammered flat to form a beautiful herringbone pattern, with a plain edge welded to either side. Such a blade was perhaps as highly valued as the gold and garnet fittings. The upper and lower guard were of gold, probably with plates of bone in between, and there were two decorated gold plates on the grip. The pommel cap of solid gold was decorated with garnets held in place by gold cell-walls carefully shaped to fit them.

A matching sword-belt also had fittings of gold and garnet, and two ornamented gold studs on the front of the scabbard held it into the belt. Two gold and garnet pyramids found to either side of the sword may have been used to adjust the tension on the sword-belt, or to ornament straps used to ensure that the sword stayed securely in its scabbard when not in use.

The helmet is ultimately derived from a late Roman cavalry helmet, with a face-plate, cheek-pieces and neck-covering. Like the shield, it may have been intended for show more than for use. The helmet was covered with tinned-bronze plaques to give a silver appearance, with the plaques stamped with a series of repeated designs. Some of these show interlaced patterns, but there is also an image (derived from a late Roman coin, but widely copied in other Germanic art) of a mounted warrior riding down a warrior on foot, and another of two dancing figures with bird-heads emerging like horns from their helmets. This design, like the helmet as a whole, has parallels in Swedish graves of the same general period. The helmet also has an iron and silver inlaid reinforcement strip over the crown, terminating above the eyes in an animal head. Another comes up to meet it and this, together with gilt eyebrows, nose and moustache, forms the shape of a bird or dragon.

Above: Iron helmet with gold and garnet decoration from a ship burial at Valsgärde, Sweden. H. 33 cm (approx.)

Above: Two silver bowls from the Sutton Hoo ship burial. Diam. 23.1 cm (max)

Eat, drink and be merry

The man in the grave was not just a warrior; apparently he knew how to throw a party. A large bronze cauldron, holding around a hundred litres, probably symbolizes his ability to feed and maintain a large war-band. In the warrior culture of the time the whole war-band would have feasted together in a great hall, and a long chain attached to the cauldron indicates that it was intended to hang in a hall of considerable size. Other smaller vessels were probably for food preparation, while jars ornamented with gilt mounts are likely to have contained food and drink.

A number of vessels of various sizes were probably used as

serving dishes. These come from a variety of sources. An ornamented bronze hanging bowl is of a typical Celtic pattern, and was probably produced in Britain, while a bronze basin came from the eastern Mediterranean. There are eleven Byzantine silver bowls and a platter which carries a stamp of the emperor Anastasius (491–518). It is recorded that silver dishes were used as imperial gifts or payments to barbarian leaders in

Left: Detail of one of the enamelled mounts on the bronze hanging bowl.

Below: Bronze hanging bowl from the Sutton Hoo ship burial. Diam. 31 cm

Above: Reconstructions of the drinking horns mounted with the original silver-gilt fittings, from the Sutton Hoo ship burial. L. 61 cm

return for military service, so this platter could easily be an heirloom from an ancestor in Roman service.

The treasures also included cups, and two great drinking horns, although only the decorative gold mounts for these survive. Finally, there are two Byzantine silver spoons. These have often been interpreted as symbolic christening spoons, since they appear to carry the Greek inscriptions SAULOS and PAULOS, taken to be a reference to St Paul. Recently, however, it has been noted that the two are not an exactly matched pair. The SAULOS spoon is of a less refined style, and may simply represent a crude copy of the PAULOS spoon. Even if they had once served as christening spoons, the symbolism was not necessarily understood at the time of the burial.

Left: Silver
platter with
stamps of
the emperor
Anastasius, from
the Sutton Hoo
ship burial.
Diam. 71.8 cm

Left: Two silver
spoons, one
apparently
inscribed
SAULOS, the
other PAULOS,
from the
Sutton Hoo
ship burial.
L 13.2 cm

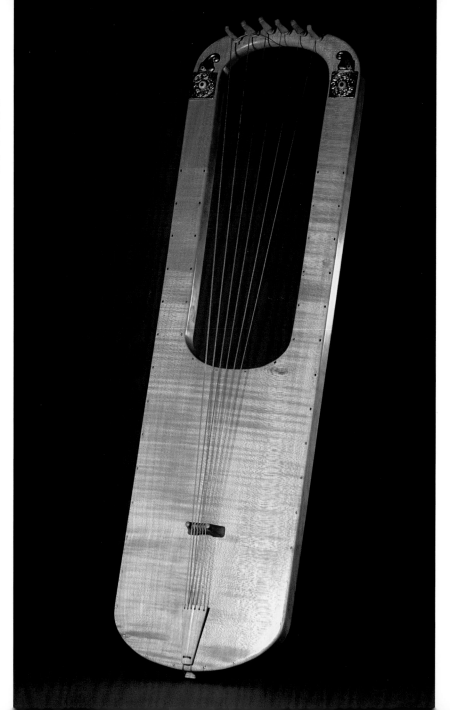

Right:
Reconstruction
of the lyre from
the Sutton Hoo
ship burial.
H. 74.5 cm

Entertainment was not limited to eating and drinking. The burial contains gaming pieces for board games, also found in other Anglo-Saxon burials. Less common, although with a few parallels, was a six-stringed wooden lyre. Only a little of the wood survived, and traces of hair attached to this showed that it had been stored in a beaver-skin bag, probably hung on the wall of the burial chamber. The lyre was ornamented with two gilt-bronze plaques, and the strings would have stretched over a bridge of bone or ivory, although this has been lost.

Below: Gilt-bronze fittings and wooden fragments from the lyre from the Sutton Hoo ship burial.

The trappings of wealth

The ship burial also contained a number of items that seem to point to personal wealth rather than a specific social status. These included textiles on the floors and walls, and buckled shoes and rich garments in or on the presumed coffin. Only traces of these remain, but several personal items of precious metal are rather better preserved.

One of the most eye-catching is the great gold belt-buckle, weighing 412.7 grams, almost exactly one Roman pound. The buckle has an intricate design of interlaced birds and beasts, with three gold bosses. Although the buckle appears solid, it is actually hollow, with a hinged back-plate and locking mechanism.

On the same belt as the great buckle was an impressive purse. The lid was a plate of bone or ivory, set into a gold frame with a

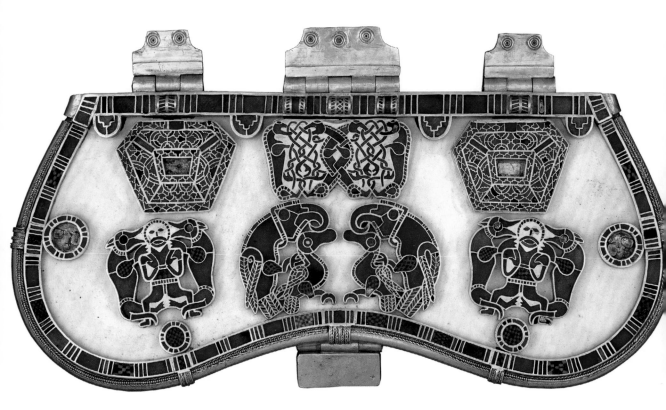

Above: Gold purse-lid, decorated with cloisonné garnets and millefiori glass, from the Sutton Hoo ship burial. L. 19 cm

sliding catch, and decorated with gold and garnet mounts. The purse contained thirty-seven gold coins called *tremisses*, three coin-shaped blanks and two small gold bars. The gold *tremisses* are all Frankish, and date to the late sixth and early seventh centuries (see p. 40). When the ship burial was found, such coins were rare in East Anglia, and the coins were interpreted as a symbolic payment for passage to the afterlife. More recent finds

show that such coins were much more common than previously thought, and they now seem more likely simply to represent the wealth of their owner.

There are several other ornaments, the most striking of which are two gold shoulder-clasps decorated with garnet and millefiori glass, both hinged around central locking pins. The clasps are derived from Roman prototypes, and may well have held together heavy fabric or padded garment. They indicate great personal wealth, but they may also have been symbols of military or royal status.

Below: Gold coins and ingots from the Sutton Hoo ship burial.

Left: Gold shoulder-clasps, decorated with cloisonné garnets and millefiori glass, from the Sutton Hoo ship burial. L. 12.7 cm

Symbols of a king

Two other items in particular have also been interpreted as symbols of royal status. A large iron stand may have been a royal standard, and perhaps had textiles suspended from the upper 'cage' section. The Venerable Bede refers to King Edwin of Northumbria (625–33) processing with a form of standard called a *tufa* by the Romans and a *tuf* by the Anglo-Saxons. A design on Anglo-Saxon coins of the later seventh century has also been interpreted as the top of a similar standard.

The other item is a stone rod, which has been interpreted as both a whetstone for sharpening swords, and as a sceptre. The rod has four human faces carved into it at each end, and one end was also mounted with an iron ring, with a bronze stag on top of the ring. The stag is probably British workmanship, but the faces may be Anglo-Saxon (although there are no direct parallels), so the two did not necessarily always belong together.

A whetstone as a symbol of power fits with the Germanic idea of the lord providing swords as rewards to his loyal warriors. Miniature whetstones were sometimes worn as pendants, presumably as symbols of power. At the same time, sceptres were used as symbols of authority in the late Roman Empire. Like so many other items in the grave, the whetstone could have functioned as a symbol of power on more than one level, reflecting both Anglo-Saxon and Roman identities.

Right: Sceptre from the Sutton Hoo ship burial. L. (whetstone) 58.3 cm

CHAPTER 4

WHO WAS BURIED AT SUTTON HOO?

The fact that no body was found in the Sutton Hoo ship burial is a mystery that has puzzled people since its first discovery in 1939, but even then the excavators realized that the body might simply have disappeared in the acidic soil. Other burials on the site contained 'sand bodies', created by reaction between the corpses and the surrounding sand. However, the wooden ship would have retained rainwater, creating a sort of acid bath in which the body could have dissolved completely.

Scientific advances since 1939 have made it possible to analyze the soil in the centre of the grave. Chemical differences between this area and the rest of the grave leave little doubt that there was originally a body, but that it eventually completely dissolved into the soil.

Another question that is often raised is whether or not this was a Christian burial. The early seventh century spans the period in which Christianity spread through southern England, beginning in Kent around 595. Since this was one of the key themes recorded in Bede's *Ecclesiastical History of England,* written just over a century later, a clear picture of the religious context of the burial might help us to date it more precisely.

Above: Details of the inscriptions from the two spoons.

Unfortunately, the picture is not clear. The coins contain Christian imagery, but that reflects the situation in Francia, where they were made, rather than in East Anglia. However, since the production of coins was closely associated in this period with Christian kingship, the fact that there are no locally produced coins in the purse suggests that these were probably not yet being made at the time of the burial, and that East Anglia was not yet Christian.

The other items of particular Christian significance were the SAULOS/PAULOS spoons. As mentioned on page 28, it is not clear that these were intended to have different inscriptions. Again, even if these were interpreted as Christian items, it tells us more about their production than it necessarily does about the burial. There is nothing locally produced in the grave that points strongly to this being a Christian grave.

It is often argued that non-Christian burials contained grave-goods, but that Christian graves did not. This is not true, as there was a long transition. A burial at Prittlewell in Essex is of comparable date to Sutton Hoo, but contains more obviously Christian items (see pages 44 and 45). As late as 685, even St Cuthbert, bishop of Lindisfarne, was buried with rich textiles and a gold and garnet cross. There is no reason why the Sutton Hoo burial could not be that of a Christian man whose followers had not yet abandoned traditional ways.

Another piece of dating evidence comes from the coins. Few of these can be precisely dated, although a coin of Theodobert II (*r*. 595–612) gives 595 as the earliest possible date for the burial. There was a gradual decline in the gold content of Frankish coins in the seventh century, and metal analysis of the Sutton Hoo coins in the 1970s led to the interpretation that the coins pointed to a burial date of around 625. This was supported by comparison with finds of Frankish coins in hoards on the Continent.

More recent work on the coinage suggests a more cautious approach to the dating. It seems unlikely that the latest coins in the hoard could date from any earlier than *c*. 610, or much later than *c*. 635. Since imported coins were still coming into East Anglia after that date, and local coins began to be produced soon after, it is likely that the burial falls between those dates.

The recent discovery of the Staffordshire hoard (see pages 44 and 46), which contained parts of over eighty high-status swords, makes us question whether all high-status objects were necessarily royal. Even so, the unusual wealth of the Sutton Hoo ship burial, the breadth of the international connections, and particularly the whetstone/sceptre, all point to a royal burial.

The favourite candidate has always been Rædwald, who died around 625, and who briefly converted to Christianity, before changing his mind. He also had the status of over-king of much of England, which fits well with the early view that the objects in the burial indicated exceptional status. In the light of more recent discoveries a lesser king also seems possible.

Rædwald still holds a central place in the possible dating of the burial to *c*. 610–35, but there are other possibilities. Rædwald's son and heir Rægenhere was killed in *c*. 617. Another son, Eorpwald, inherited from his father and later converted to Christianity, but was killed shortly after, around 627, by a pagan called Ricberht. After this, East Anglia reverted to paganism for three years, possibly under Ricberht's rule. Nothing else is known about him, including whether or not he was a family member.

A brother or half-brother of Eorpwald, Sigeberht, became king around this time, but retired to a monastery around 634, leaving the kingdom in the hands of his kinsman Ecgric, but both were killed not long afterwards when East Anglia was invaded.

Any one of these rulers might be the man buried in Mound 1 at Sutton Hoo. Rædwald remains the preferred choice, if only because he is better known than the other candidates. The truth is that without new evidence, we will never know for certain who was buried at Sutton Hoo.

Above and left: Gold *tremissis* of the Frankish king Theodobert II (*r.* AD 595–612), from the Sutton Hoo ship burial. Diam. 1.25 cm

CHAPTER 5
OTHER IMPORTANT FINDS

The Sutton Hoo ship burial stands out as the most important Anglo-

Saxon find of the period. Even so, to understand it, archaeologists

have to look at other finds as well.

Below: Pair of drinking horns with silver-gilt mounts from the princely burial at Taplow, Buckinghamshire. L. 44.5 cm

A number of high-status burials were discovered in the nineteenth century, and knowledge of these helped Basil Brown and his successors to interpret Sutton Hoo. Snape, near Aldeburgh (just a few miles from Sutton Hoo), was excavated in 1862. Like at Sutton Hoo, there was a cemetery of several burial mounds, and the largest of these contained a ship around fifteen metres long. The mound had been looted, but a few remaining grave-goods showed that this was a sixth-century Anglo-Saxon burial.

A seventh-century male burial was uncovered at Benty Grange in Derbyshire in 1848. This included decorative mountings from a cup, together with personal ornaments and armour. The most significant find was the remains of a helmet, which survived as an iron frame, with a gilt-bronze boar as a crest. The gaps between the frame would have been filled with horn or leather.

A princely burial dating from the seventh century was uncovered at Taplow in Buckinghamshire in 1883, although the finds were only fully interpreted in the light of Sutton Hoo. Taplow provides many parallels to the Sutton Hoo ship burial, including a beautiful gold and garnet belt-buckle, weapons, a lyre, gaming board and pieces, at least nineteen decorated vessels for eating and drinking, and rich textiles. The burial was apparently not quite as rich as that at Sutton Hoo, but it still represents the top level of Anglo-Saxon society, perhaps a king or chieftain who ruled a smaller area than whoever was buried at Sutton Hoo.

More recently, in 1997, a burial was discovered near Wollaston in Northamptonshire, during the extraction of gravel. As at Benty Grange, the highlight of the discovery was a boar-crested helmet. Made of undecorated iron, this is more functional than the Sutton Hoo helmet, but there are clear similarities, including protective cheek-pieces.

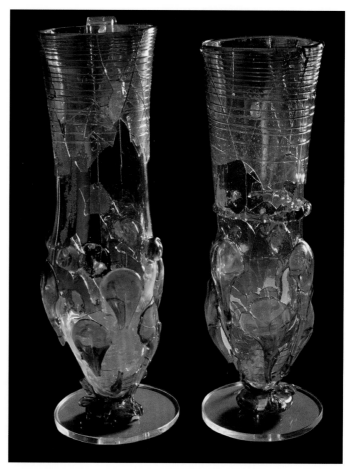

Above: Glass claw beakers from the princely burial at Taplow, Buckinghamshire. H. 30.1 cm (max)

In 2003, a burial chamber was discovered during road building at Prittlewell, on the outskirts of Southend in Essex. An Anglo-Saxon cemetery was already known there, but the new find provides one of the closest parallels to Sutton Hoo, containing weapons, a lyre and gaming pieces, vessels for food and drink, a gold buckle, coins and a curious iron stand. Like the burial at Taplow, it is very high status, but not quite as rich as Sutton Hoo.

A very different find was discovered by a metal detectorist in 2009. The 'Staffordshire hoard' contained many gold and silver fragments, but was not a human burial. Most of the items identified so far are decorative fittings from weapons and other war-gear, including pieces of at least two helmets and over eighty swords, similar in style and status to the Sutton Hoo sword. The hoard also included gold crosses.

Above: Iron helmet from a
burial at Wollaston,
Northamptonshire.
H. 36 cm (approx.)

Right: Gold crosses from a burial at
Prittlewell, Essex. H. c. 3 cm

Above: Reconstruction drawing
of the burial chamber at Prittlewell,
Essex.

Below: A selection of gold and garnet pieces from the spectacular Staffordshire Hoard, discovered in 2009.

The most likely explanation seems to be that this was carefully selected loot from defeated enemies. The symbolic destruction of these high-status items provides a mirror to the preservation of such items in the Sutton Hoo ship burial and other graves.

CHAPTER 6

SUTTON HOO TODAY

In 1998 the site at Sutton Hoo was donated by the Annie Tranmer Charitable Trust to the National Trust. The grave-field is open to the public, and it is also possible to visit Mrs Pretty's house.

A visitor centre has been established, and this contains a permanent display on the ship burial, and on other archaeological features spanning the centuries of human activity on the site. The display includes a mixture of replicas from the Sutton Hoo ship burial, and genuine finds from some of the excavations. Digging in preparation for the visitor centre revealed a second Anglo-Saxon cemetery five hundred metres to the north of the Sutton Hoo mounds, slightly earlier and not as wealthy.

In addition to the permanent facilities, the visitor centre houses a temporary exhibition space. The British Museum makes regular loans from its collection, including selections from the Mound 1 ship burial and other supporting material. Not only does this allow Mrs Pretty's gift to the nation to be seen in Suffolk as well as London, but it allows the visitor centre to create different themed exhibitions each year on the many different stories that the Sutton Hoo treasures still have to tell.

FURTHER READING

Alexander, M. (transl.), *Beowulf,* Penguin (1973)

Bruce-Mitford, R.L.S., *The Sutton Hoo Ship Burial,* 3 vols, British Museum Press (1975, 1978, 1983)

Carver, M.O.H. (ed.), *The Age of Sutton Hoo,* Boydell (1992)

Carver, M.O.H., *Sutton Hoo: Burial ground of kings?,* British Museum Press (1998)

Carver, M.O.H. (ed.), *Sutton Hoo: A seventh-century princely burial ground and its context,* British Museum Press/Society of Antiquaries of London (2005)

Evans, A., *The Sutton Hoo Ship Burial,* British Museum Press (1994, repr. 2008)

Hirst, S., *The Prittlewell Prince. The discovery of a rich Anglo-Saxon burial in Essex,* Museum of London (2004)

Kendall, C.B., & Wells, P.S. (ed.), *Voyage to the Other World,* University of Minnesota Press (1992)

Leahy, K & Bland, R., *The Staffordshire Hoard,* British Museum Press (2009)

Marzinzik, S., *The Sutton Hoo Helmet,* British Museum Press (2007)

Williams, G., *Early Anglo-Saxon Coins,* Shire Books (2008)

PICTURE CREDITS